23.—

Dance
FOR FUN!

By Balinda Craig-Quijada

Content Adviser: Noel Reiss, Lecturer, Department of Dance and Theater, UNC Charlotte
Reading Adviser: Frances J. Bonacci, Reading Specialist, Cambridge, Massachusetts

COMPASS POINT BOOKS

MINNEAPOLIS, MINNESOTA

Compass Point Books
3109 West 50th Street, #115
Minneapolis, MN 55410

Visit Compass Point Books on the Internet at *www.compasspointbooks.com*
or e-mail your request to *custserv@compasspointbooks.com*

Photographs ©: Rubberball Productions, front cover (left), 11 (center), 15, 23, 36; Ron Leighton, front cover (top right), 11 (bottom left), 43; PhotoDisc, front cover (bottom right), 11 (bottom right), 23, 42, 44 (bottom), 45 (top); Digital Vision, 5; Hulton Archive, 7; Corel, 9, 45 (bottom); Photos.com, 10; Ariel Skelley/Corbis, 13; Eyewire, 11 (top left), 47; Ingram Publishing, 11 (top right), 43 (left); Kwame Zikomo/SuperStock, 17; Jade Albert Studios Inc./Getty Images, 19; Larry Williams/Corbis, 27; Jim Erickson/Corbis, 31; Lisette Le Bon/SuperStock, 33; Stephen Simpson/Getty Images, 35; Peter Beavis/Getty Images, 39; PhotoSpin, 41.

Editor: Sandra E. Will/Bill SMITH STUDIO
Photo Researchers: Sandra E. Will and Christie Silver/Bill SMITH STUDIO
Designer: Colleen Sweet and Brian Kobberger/Bill SMITH STUDIO

Library of Congress Cataloging-in-Publication Data
Craig-Quijada, Balinda.
Dance for fun / by Balinda Craig-Quijada.
p. cm. — (Activities for fun)
Includes index.
Summary: A survey of dance, including tap, modern, jazz, and ballet, and a timeline of the history of dance and the place it holds in cultures around the world.
ISBN 0-7565-0587-9 (hardcover)
1. Dance—Juvenile literature. [1. Dance.] I. Title. II. Series.
GV1596.5.C73 2004
792.8—dc22

2003016721

Table of Contents

Note: In this book, there are two kinds of vocabulary words. Dance Words to Know are words specific to dance. They are in **bold** and are defined on page 46. Other Words to Know are helpful words that aren't related only to dance. They are ***bold and italicized.*** These are defined on page 47.

Dance Is Fun

Do you listen to your favorite music and find you cannot sit still? You just want to tap your foot. Soon, you have to stand up and move, sway back and forth, or jump up and down. When you feel the **rhythm** of the music and start moving, you are dancing. The speed, or **tempo,** of the music can decide how fast or slowly you move. No one has to teach you how to do this kind of dancing.

Other types of dance must be done a certain way and require training and practice. Dance can include almost any kind of movement and express any kind of mood. All types of dance have one thing in common: people like to move their bodies. It just feels good.

Dance is a way to have fun with old friends, meet new friends, or celebrate happy times like weddings. Dance is creative. Dance is social. Dance can be art, too. No matter how old you are, dance is fun and has something to offer everyone!

Through the Centuries

Dance has existed for thousands of years. People all over the world dance, and the art of dance has played an important role in many cultures throughout history. Some people dance to celebrate special events, like a birth or a death. Special dances have also honored kings, queens, and emperors in countries like France and Japan.

Dance is always shifting and changing. Social dances, the kind done by average people as part of having fun, spread quickly from one place to another. The **waltz** was a very popular partner dance in Europe in the 1800s that soon came to the United States. In the 1920s, a crazy dance called the **charleston** was popular across the United States. **Break dancing** started with teenagers in New York City and spread all over the world during the 1970s and 1980s.

Today's hip-hop (see p. 38) came from break dancing. Hip-hoppers still do some of the same moves break dancers did, such as head spins, flips, and the moonwalk. They have added their own moves, too.

Dance is often passed along like this from **generation** to generation with each new group adding its own style to the form.

Siblings James F. and Louise Sullivan dance the charleston at the 1926 National Charleston Championship. They won the competition.

From Africa to Europe

Every culture has its own types of dances. Most are accompanied by music. Some require years of training to perform them well.

Spanish flamenco dancers use hard-soled shoes, fast-moving steps, and **castanets** to create complex rhythms and dramatic moves. Chinese opera dancers are *acrobatic* and use colorful makeup and singing to tell stories. Sacred temple dances performed in India and Bali require dancers to learn special ways to dance. They use their hands, fingers, and even their faces to tell grand stories of gods and warriors.

For many African cultures, dance is an important part of everyday life. Dance in Africa is closely connected to drumming. African dancers learn to play the drums so that they understand the dance rhythms. In Africa, dance is performed by all the people who come to an event.

The fanga from the African country Nigeria is a dance of welcoming that was first performed when visitors to Nigeria arrived on ships.

No matter where people live, dance is a way for them to come together, celebrate, and express themselves.

An Indian woman performs a religious dance at a temple in Mahabalipuram, India.

In Costume

Dancers often wear costumes when they perform. Some are quite detailed. In a famous ballet called "Afternoon of a Fawn," the dancer's fawn costume looks to be part human and part deer as he leaps and prances through an imaginary forest.

Masks are very important in some dances to tell stories. Pacific Northwest Indians have created wonderful wooden masks to represent powerful characters and birds in their *mythology.*

Other parts of the costume include makeup and props like finger cymbals, fans, castanets, swords, and scarves.

When practicing ballet or modern dance, dancers wear a **leotard** with tights underneath. Some dancers even wear a **unitard.** Female ballet dancers also often wear a wrap skirt or leggings over their tights while they practice. This helps to keep their muscles warm.

Shoes are important in dance, too. Ballet dance requires specially designed shoes that help dancers stand on their toes. Tap dancers' shoes have metal taps attached near the toes and at the heels to make clicking sounds while they dance.

Training Time

How do people learn how to dance well? They take many classes and spend a lot of time practicing. Dance studios, or schools, offer a large selection of classes for people of all ages and skill levels.

You can start taking classes at any age, but some students start studying dance as young as 5 years old. Many dancers begin ballet as young as 3 or 4 to build the muscles and strength they need. Dancers start at the beginning level and move on to the intermediate level. Students usually move from beginning to intermediate level in one or two years. It can take many years of study to reach an advanced level of dance.

If you want to take dance lessons, you will probably find that most of the classes offered are in one of these forms: ballet, jazz, tap, or modern. Most dance classes meet twice a week and last for one to two hours. At the end of each year, most schools have a recital where students can show what they have learned to an audience of family and friends.

Ballet

Ballet is a very old form of dance. It began in France in the court of King Louis XIV during the 1600s. Dance was an important part of life in the court. Kings, queens, princes, and princesses practiced to become good dancers. It was a way to entertain and impress each other and to honor the king.

Over the years, ballet spread from the courts of kings to the stage. Ballet was performed by ***professional*** dancers who trained at academies, or schools, for dance. Most professional dancers performed with companies that toured all over the world. Touring European companies and **soloists** brought ballet to the United States. By the late 18th century, several dancers had moved from Europe to the United States and started their own ballet schools.

This dancer is doing a passé. Because ballet began in France, the names of the ballet steps have remained in French. Ballet dancers can take a class anywhere in the world and understand the names of the steps.

Beginning in the early 20th century, ballet became a serious form of art in the United States with performances featuring famous dancers like Anna Pavlova and Fanny Elssler. Russian-born dancer Mikhail Baryshnikov became one of the most popular ballet dancers of the 20th century. Many people consider Baryshnikov to be one of the greatest dancers of all time. His dancing has inspired a new generation of *premiere* ballet dancers.

How to Do It

Much of the movement in ballet begins with special positions, or ways to hold the body. There are positions for the feet, for the arms, for the legs, and even for the head. The positions help to create long lines in space that stretch from a dancer's fingers to the toes. Ballet dancers learn to look like they are light and elegant, almost as if they can float through the air.

One way to make dancers look light and beautiful is to have the women dance *en pointe* (on-pwont). That is a French term meaning "on the tips of the toes." To dance en pointe, dancers need specially designed pointe shoes and many years of training to strengthen the muscles of their feet and legs.

Dancers must be able to dance at an intermediate or advanced level before they begin dancing en pointe. Also, most girls do not dance en pointe until they are in their early teens because they can cause damage to their growing bones.

Ballet dancers never stop taking classes to improve and practice their **techniques.** Class begins with the dancers standing at the *barre* (bar), which is a long railing made of wood attached to the wall. A mirror at the front of the room lets dancers see exactly how their bodies are working. Ballet dancers spend a lot of time practicing to improve and perfect their skill.

*Dancers hold the barre with one hand and do exercises that warm up the body and strengthen the muscles of the feet, legs, hips, and **torso**.*

And All That Jazz

Fast, sharp, and lively, jazz dancing is very popular and has many influences. Jazz dance traces its roots to Africa. When slaves were taken to the United States from Africa, they brought their ***traditional*** dances. Over time, these dances mixed with European dances and influenced many social dances in the United States. As these dances were passed on through generations, they changed and included many elements from other dances.

Jazz dance as we know it today began with ragtime and jazz music during the early 1900s. The city of New Orleans was the home of this new kind of music. Horns, clarinets, banjoes, and pianos played lively tunes throughout the city. Jazz dancers soon performed in big shows that traveled across the country and included music, comedy, and dancing. These variety shows were called vaudeville. Jazz dance borrowed steps from popular social dances with animal and food names like the monkey, the pony, the chicken, and the mashed potato.

Jazz is a dance form that constantly changes, depending on the music that is popular at the time. Jazz dance teachers help students learn fast turns, high kicks, big leaps, and snappy head and hip movements. You can see some examples of the many styles of jazz dance on Broadway stages and in music videos.

Jazz dancers try to show the rhythms and feelings of the music through their movement.

How to Do It

A main feature of jazz dance is a technique called **isolation**—moving the head, feet, hips, or arms independently of each other in different tempos at the same time. For example, your feet may be walking on the beat of the music, while your arms and hips move much more quickly or more slowly. Here are some of the isolation exercises that jazz dancers use:

Jazz hands: Open your hands with your fingers spread, sending the energy out through your hands.

Shoulders: Shrug your right shoulder up by your ear, then let it drop. Repeat with your left shoulder. Make a "square" with your shoulder—move it forward, move it up by the ear, move it back, return to center.

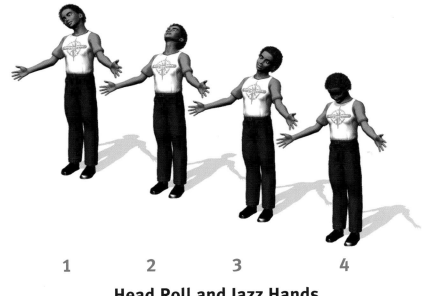

1 2 3 4

Head Roll and Jazz Hands

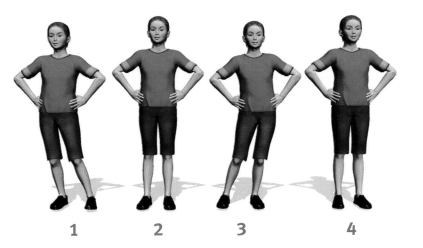

1 2 3 4

Hips

Head: Moving your head only, look right and return to front, then look left and return to front. Look up, return to front, look down, return to front. Move your ear to your right shoulder, then return to the front. Next, do the same thing with your left ear. Roll your head (pictured) around after doing your isolations, like you are drawing a big circle on the ceiling with the top of your head.

Hips: Move your hips right (1), center (2), left (3), center (4). Then, move forward (tuck hips under), center, back (sway back), center. Try circling your hips smoothly (like you are stirring a bowl with your hips) forward, right side, back, left side. Repeat.

Stomp!

Making rhythms with the feet is what tap dance is all about. With the help of metal plates, called **taps,** attached to their shoes, tap dancers click, drag, and stomp endless combinations of rhythms. Tap dancers add their tapping to the music like an extra set of drums.

The best tap dancers do a lot of **improvisation.** There are various styles of tap dancing, too. In **softshoe,** the performer often sings or even performs a bit of comedy as he or she dances. Broadway tap is quick and light and often involves big groups of dancers all tapping at once. Fred Astaire, one of the most famous tap dancers of the 20th century, featured softshoe and Broadway tap in many of his movies.

Rhythm tap is all about noise and speed. Heavy, bold stomping uses every part of the foot and shoe. Savion Glover, who has appeared on "Sesame Street" and in the musical "Bring in 'da Noise, Bring in 'da Funk," is a rhythm tapper.

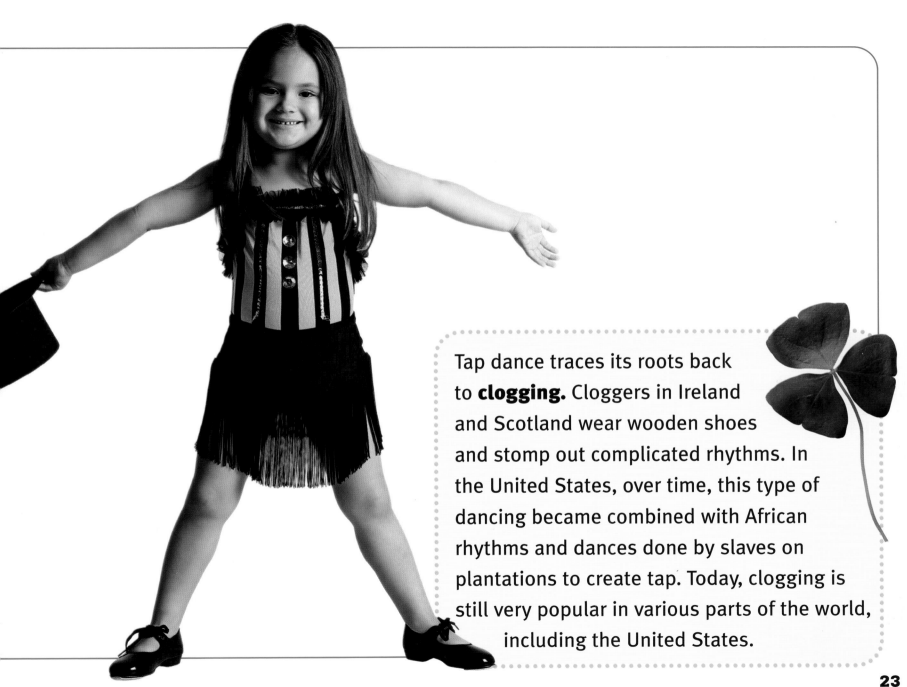

Tap dance traces its roots back to **clogging.** Cloggers in Ireland and Scotland wear wooden shoes and stomp out complicated rhythms. In the United States, over time, this type of dancing became combined with African rhythms and dances done by slaves on plantations to create tap. Today, clogging is still very popular in various parts of the world, including the United States.

How to Do It

While improvisation is a big part of good tap dancing, there are basic steps to learn first. Training helps develop looseness in the ankle, allowing tappers to bang out very fast, clear sounds and rhythms. Students of tap learn to make a clear sound with each part of the foot and shoe. As soon as a new tapper has some control of the sounds his or her shoes make, simple rhythms and "time steps" can be created and practiced.

Call-and-response is one of the most fun exercises in a tap class. One tapper creates a rhythm. Then, the other tappers respond by adding their own tapping as if they have been asked a question and are answering. The rhythm grows more complicated and interesting as various dancers add their own ideas. Here are some basic tap exercises:

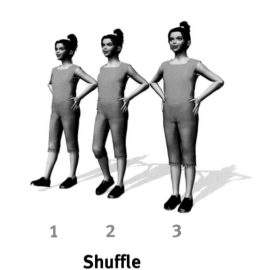

Shuffle

1   2   3

Shuffle: Makes two sounds. First, brush forward with the ball of the foot, tapping your heel. Then, pull back with the ball of the foot, tapping your toe. Finally, stand with your feet together.

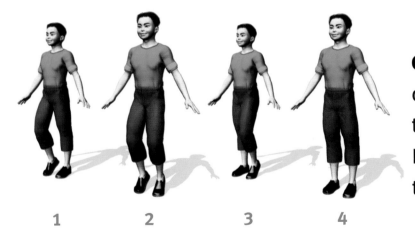

1   2   3   4

Cramp Roll

Cramp roll: Makes four quick sounds. In quick *succession,* step up on the ball of the right foot, then the ball of the left foot. Next, drop the heel of the right foot, then the left foot.

Something New

Modern dance began in the United States in the early 1900s. The pioneers of modern dance had grown tired of the strict rules of ballet dancing. They wanted to dance in a more free and creative way. They wanted to make up dances that could be angry, happy, sad, ugly, or beautiful. They also wanted to create dances that were seen as important works of art, like the paintings of Pablo Picasso or books by famous authors. Until modern dance, only ballet was considered an "important" form of dance. Other dance was only considered to be entertainment.

Modern dancers developed new ways to train the body to move, and they had new ideas about what a dance should do. Many of the dances performed by modern dancers are *abstract*. Instead of telling a story, abstract dance explores the shapes human bodies can make and all the different ways that dancers can move with one another.

Unlike some other dance forms, modern dance encourages dancers to explore and create new movements.

How to Do It

There are many styles of modern dance, but they have some things in common. Modern dancers are taught to be very aware of how gravity, or force, affects the way they move. They even learn to be aware of how they breathe when they dance.

Modern dancers train for many years to make their bodies *flexible* and strong. Many take other kinds of movement classes to help prepare their bodies to do the widest range of movement. They might take classes in **yoga,** ballet, **tai chi,** or even **capoeira,** an acrobatic combination of dance and the martial arts.

Modern dancers prepare to do whatever a **choreographer** asks for—a handstand, baseball slide, lifting a partner, or somersaults. Movements like the forward swing help dancers to properly warm up their muscles and spine before they do more advanced moves.

Forward Swing: Raise your arms straight above your head (being careful not to raise your shoulders). Then, reach your arms forward as you let your arms and chest swing forward and down. Your arms should make a big circle like the arms of a clock. Next, you rebound at the bottom of the swing with a bounce in your knees and retrace your path as you return to standing position. With the right speed and rebound, this move feels like you are on a swingset!

1   2   3   4   5

Forward Swing

Join the Party!

Some forms of dance do not require special training like ballet, tap, jazz, and modern do. Social dance is a way to have fun with friends, release energy, and further enjoy the music you are listening to. Places where you can social dance include weddings, parties, school dances, **discotheques,** street dances, and even your own living room!

Social dances can be done with a partner, in a group, or alone. There are country western line dances, and line dances like the electric slide. For this dance, people line up in rows on the dance floor and perform a series of movements together, while the DJ plays the song "The Electric Slide." Other dances, like the macarena and the hokey pokey, are named after popular songs and are performed by big groups of people at social dances.

Regardless of the type of music people like, social dancing has something fun to offer for everyone.

Around the Floor

Have you ever watched a dance competition on television? If so, you have probably seen people perform **ballroom** dancing.

Ballroom dancing is the most well-known form of partner dance. In the early 20th century, ballroom dance started as a way to bring *sophistication* and grace to the social dancing done in dance halls. Vernon and Irene Castle became one of the first famous ballroom dance couples. They opened a school in New York in 1914 to teach elegance and good manners through dancing. Ordinary people flocked to ballroom dancing classes to learn stylish dances like the tango, fox trot, and cha-cha-cha.

During the 20th century, the popularity of ballroom dance continued to grow. Today, many couples participate in ballroom dance competitions all over the world. Competitive dancers have to master all of the ballroom dances in two categories: standard and Latin American. Couples do the tango, Viennese waltz, slow fox trot, and quickstep in the standard category.

The samba, cha-cha-cha, rumba, *paso doble*, and jive make up the Latin American category.

At competitions, dozens of couples fly around the dance floor at once and try to catch the eye of the judges with their sharp dancing and elaborate, colorful costumes.

Jump and Jive

Like ballroom dancing, swing dance is a popular form of partner dance. Swing is a fast-paced and lively dance style that first became popular in the 1920s and '30s during the big band era. The music from orchestras led by Count Basie, Duke Ellington, and many others inspired swing dancers all over the United States.

Like swing music, swing dance is energetic and fast. Swing has many different styles, like the lindy hop, jitterbug, and east coast swing. The type of swing dance a couple might perform depends on the rhythm of the music.

Most swing dancers go to special clubs or dance halls that feature swing music. Many swing dancers dress in clothing styles that were popular during the big band era when they go out dancing. Each couple tries to show off their moves and their fashion sense while they are out spinning, flipping, and leaping across the dance floor.

Olé!

Originally from Latin America, salsa became popular in the United States during the 1940s and '50s. At that time, big band music from Cuba was being played in clubs in New York. People became introduced to salsa through the new music.

Salsa dance is a couple dance. Like swing dance, salsa has a basic foot pattern rhythm that can go forward and back, or side to side. While on the dance floor, salsa dancers feel the music together, and they let the music guide them in the steps and rhythm they create.

Salsa is known for its upbeat music and quick footwork and turns. In salsa, dancers create a lot of their movements by keeping their hips moving, which is very important.

Salsa is especially popular in Latin American countries, certain regions of the United States, and Europe. Dancers have fun moving to the music in lively and loud social clubs, parties, and discos!

Salsa has branched out into many related forms of music and dance, including mambo, rumba, and cha-cha-cha.

Hip-Hop Hooray!

Can you hip-hop? Hip-hop dance began as entertainment in the streets of the South Bronx in New York City. Then, it spread worldwide through music videos. Hip-hop is a **collage** of different dance styles ranging from disco, rhythm-and-blues, and reggae, to capoeira and break dance.

Hip-hop dance can be very acrobatic. While a DJ spins records on a turntable, scratching and **sampling** various pieces of music together, dancers may spin on top of their heads or do crazy flips. Hip-hop dancing usually takes place in a circle with participants dancing on the sidelines. The dancers all take turns doing solos in the middle to show off their latest moves. Hip-hop dancers often compete in a game of "oneupsmanship," where they try to outdo and impress each other with their moves. They usually save their best moves until they see the other dancers' best moves.

Good hip-hop dancers develop their own special moves. They are always looking for new steps to borrow and make part of their style.

Hip-hop dancers often give themselves nicknames that describe what they look like when they dance, such as rubberband or crazylegs.

Festivals and More

Cultural dancing is an important part of many groups. Most types of folk dancing are performed at festivals or special occasions, such as weddings.

Some types of folk dancing and native dancing are passed down from generation to generation. Native Americans perform dances like the hoop dance and the eagle dance at their get-togethers, or powwows. Folk dances and native dances are usually taught to children by older members of their family or tribe. The Israeli dance called the *hora* is a celebration dance performed at Jewish weddings.

Other types of folk or cultural dancing require special classes. Irish step dancing is a complicated form of dancing that became popular in the United States during the 1990s. Many places in the United States and around the world have special step dancing schools, where dancers can learn the difficult steps and patterns.

Festivals provide a fun way for people of all cultures to dance and celebrate.

Dance Timeline

What Happened When?

| 1651 | 1850 | 1870 | 1890 | 1930 | 1940 | 1950 | 1960 |

1651 King Louis XIV of France performs as a dancer for the first time at age 13. Two years later, he portrays the rising sun. He is soon known as "The Sun King."

1850s Irish jigs are combined with African-American dances to form tap dance.

1877 Modern dance pioneer Isadora Duncan is born.

1892 Lev Ivanov choreographs "The Nutcracker Suite" to Tchaikovsky's classical music score.

1928 Tapper Bill "Bojangles" Robinson becomes the first African-American dancing star on Broadway. He performs his signature "stair dance."

1930s Early modern dance pioneers like Martha Graham and Doris Humphrey explore more creative ways of moving.

Martha Graham ➤

1934 Fred Astaire and Ginger Rogers dance together in the movie "The Gay Divorcée." Their tap and ballroom routines remain among the best and most beloved dance captured on film.

1944 Martha Graham's "Appalachian Spring" debuts. The dance, with a score by composer Aaron Copland, helps establish modern dance as an art form.

1960 Alvin Ailey choreographs "Revelations," set to the music of black spirituals.

1962 The Judson Dance Theater is created in New York City. It becomes the place where modern dancers, painters, and musicians gather to experiment with new art forms. Their work comes to be called "postmodern."

1962 Broadway choreographer Jerome Robbins recreates the musical "West Side Story" for the movies.

1970	1980	1990	2000

1968 Arthur Mitchell forms the Dance Theater of Harlem. His goal was to give African-American dancers opportunities to excel in classical ballet.

1980s Hip-hop emerges in constantly changing forms that include breaking, pop and lock, and b-boy, among others.

1996 "Riverdance" is performed at Radio City Music Hall in New York City following a popular run in Dublin, Ireland. A skilled group of Irish dancers make step dancing popular in the United States.

1983 "Flashdance," a movie featuring funky jazz dance, is a big hit.

1974 Ballet dance sensation Mikhail Baryshnikov, the greatest male ballet dancer of the 20th century, leaves the Soviet Union and comes to the United States.

1983 "A Chorus Line," a musical that features flashy dance numbers, becomes the longest running musical in Broadway history.

2002 "Chicago," a Bob Fosse Broadway musical, becomes an Oscar-winning film. It helps make the movie musical popular again.

2003 Choreographer Twyla Tharp wins Broadway's Tony Award for "Movin' Out." In the musical, dancers perform to the music of Billy Joel for the entire show.

1977 Disco dancing is all the rage. Ranging from couple dances like the hustle, to line dances like the bus stop, the fad moves from clubs in New York City and Los Angeles to the rest of the country.

1996 "Bring in 'da Noise, Bring in 'da Funk," Savion Glover's tap dance explosion, hits the Broadway stage and wins four Tony Awards.

1996 The macarena latin dance craze hits the United States.

2004 DanceSport, a form of ballroom dancing, is featured for the first time at the Summer Olympic Games.

Dance Trivia

The charleston, a popular dance craze of the 1920s, is thought to have originated with the Ashanti people of Africa. African slaves who lived on an island off of Charleston, South Carolina, probably brought the original steps to the United States.

Before today's sturdy pointe shoe was developed, early ballerinas put cardboard in their shoes to help support them while they danced on their toes.

Tappers looking for new sounds create "jingle" taps by placing a washer between the metal tap and the sole of the shoe. Others may spread sand on the floor to add a swishing or scraping sound to their tapping.

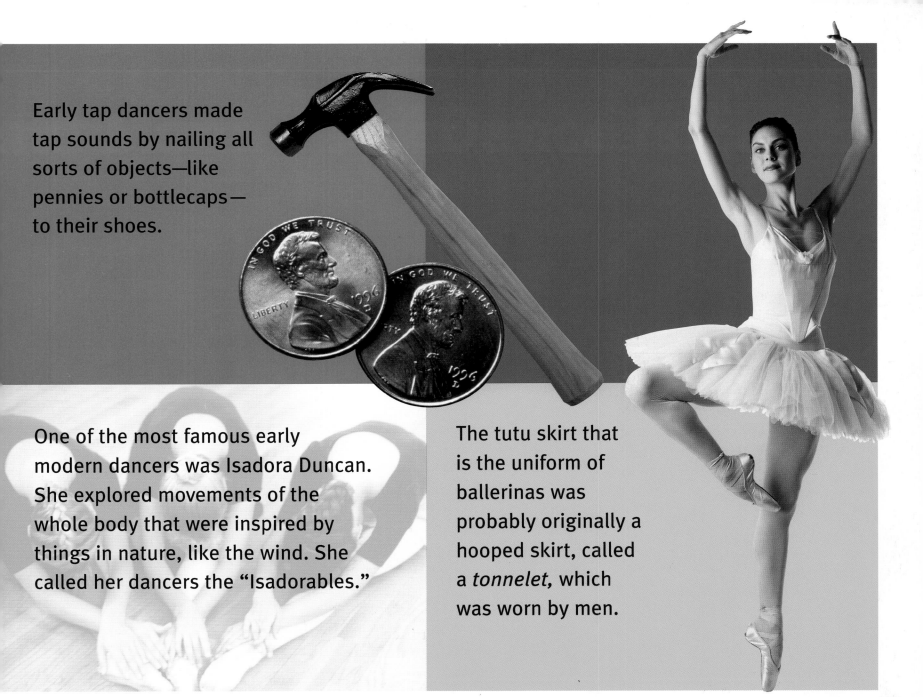

Early tap dancers made tap sounds by nailing all sorts of objects—like pennies or bottlecaps—to their shoes.

One of the most famous early modern dancers was Isadora Duncan. She explored movements of the whole body that were inspired by things in nature, like the wind. She called her dancers the "Isadorables."

The tutu skirt that is the uniform of ballerinas was probably originally a hooped skirt, called a *tonnelet,* which was worn by men.

Dance Words to Know

ballroom: a large room made for dancing

break dancing: a combination of dance and acrobatic moves that originated on the streets of the South Bronx in New York City during the 1970s and '80s

capoeira: an acrobatic combination of dance and the martial arts invented in Brazil

castanet: a musical instrument made from two shells or pieces of wood that is held in the palm of a dancer's hand and clicked in time to the music; commonly used by flamenco dancers

charleston: a social dance originating in the 1920s that featured flapping arms and other birdlike movements

choreographer: a person who creates and directs dances

clogging: a social and competitive dance originating in Ireland; performed to Irish jigs, hornpipes, and reels by dancers wearing wooden shoes

collage: a dance that brings together parts of different dance traditions to make something new

discotheque: a dance club or place where people dance

improvisation: movement made up on the spot by one or more dancers

isolation: moving different parts of the body, such as the head, arms, and legs, independently of each other

leotard: a close-fitting one-piece article of clothing worn by dancers

rhythm: the pattern and timing of the beat in music

sampling: the borrowing of small pieces of previously recorded music from other artists when creating new music

softshoe: a form of tap dance, where the dancer sings or performs comedy while dancing

solo: when a dancer performs alone

tai chi: an ancient Chinese martial art form that features very slow movement meant to focus the mind and train the body

taps: metal plates that are attached to dance shoes; used for tap dance

technique: the skills, form, and basic physical movements that dancers work on in class

tempo: the speed of music or a dance

unitard: a close-fitting one-piece article of clothing for the torso, legs, feet, and arms

waltz: a social dance done where partners glide around the dance floor while turning gracefully with smooth steps; the dance was made popular in Vienna, Austria, during the 19th century

yoga: an ancient Hindu/Indian practice that uses a series of poses and special breathing to train and connect the mind and body

GLOSSARY
Other Words to Know

Here are definitions for some of the words used in this book:

abstract: something that does not tell a story

acrobatic: movements borrowed from gymnastics, like handstands, flips, and forward rolls

flexible: able to bend or move easily

generation: a group of people born and living at the same time

mythology: old or ancient stories told again and again that help connect people with their past

premiere: first in position, rank, or importance

professional: a person paid to do a job

sophistication: a sense of style often associated with wealthy and educated people

succession: one thing after another in order

torso: the middle of the body that includes the length of the spine, from the neck to the hips

traditional: a dance, belief, or custom handed down from one generation to the next

Where to Learn More

AT THE LIBRARY

Glover, Savion. *Savion! My Life in Tap*. New York Morrow Junior, 2000.

Grau, Dr. Andree. *Dance*. New York: DK Publishing, 2000.

Varriale, Jim. *Kids Dance: The Students of Ballet Tech*. New York Dutton Books, 1999.

ON THE ROAD

Jacob's Pillow Dance Festival
358 George Carter Road
Becket, MA 01223
413/637-1322

National Museum of Dance & Hall of Fame
99 S. Broadway
Saratoga Springs, NY 12866-9809
518/584-2225

Dance Arts Museum of the Americas
Box 118
Santa Fe, NM 87504
505/466-2891

ON THE WEB

For more information on dance, use FactHound to track down Web sites related to this book.

1. Go to www.compasspointbooks.com/facthound
2. Type in this book ID: 0756505879
3. Click on the *FETCH IT* button.

 Your trusty FactHound will fetch the best Web sites for you!

INDEX

ABOUT THE AUTHOR

Balinda Craig-Quijada is director of the dance program at Kenyon College, where she teaches modern dance, ballet, dance history, and composition. She received a B.A. in religion from the University of Iowa and a M.F.A. in dance from Ohio State University. Her pickup company, BCQ DANCE, is based in Columbus, Ohio. Craig-Quijada also performs regularly with the Columbus-based HighJinks Dance Company. She is currently a board member of the American College Dance Festival Association.